Original title:

Petals and Promises

Copyright © 2025 Creative Arts Management OÜ
All rights reserved.

Author: Colin Leclair
ISBN HARDBACK: 978-1-80581-749-9
ISBN PAPERBACK: 978-1-80581-276-0
ISBN EBOOK: 978-1-80581-749-9

### Beneath the Dew, a Promise

In the morning light, they peek,
Tiny flowers start to speak.
Whispers soft of secret cheer,
What's the joke? We're waiting here.

Little bees with buzzing quests,
Humming tunes in fuzzy vests.
They juggle pollen, oh so sly,
Crafting nectar, oh my, my!

## Blossoms Entwined in Fate

Two blooms met, a flirty dance,
Caught in springtime's wild romance.
One swayed left, the other right,
Tangled up beneath starlight.

Daisy laughed at Tulip's joke,
While Sunflower wore a cloak.
In their gossip, time flew fast,
A garden party unsurpassed!

### The Lullaby of Green Hopes

In the garden, frogs do croak,
Making music, what a joke!
Crickets chirp and steal the show,
Singing ballads soft and low.

A snail's race is quite absurd,
It takes ages to be heard.
And ladybugs play hide and seek,
By the fence, they squeak and squeak!

## Garden of Silent Reminders

A gnome sits still, his humor bright,
With a grin that gives a fright.
Rabbits bounce around his feet,
Falling over—what a treat!

While daisies gossip quite loud,
In a patch, they form a crowd.
"Did you see the way he tripped?"
Pansies chuckle, none are skipped.

## The Unseen Ties

You gave me a wink, I offered a sneeze,
A dance in the rain, slipping on peas.
Together we twirled, then fell on our backs,
With laughter that echoed, like silly sound tracks.

We share secret snacks, hidden under a chair,
Goldfish and pickles, it's quite the bizarre fare.
When the world looks askew, we giggle like kids,
Bound by our quirks, like odd little bids.

## In the Shade of Fulfilled Dreams

Under the sun, we wear mismatched shoes,
Chasing after ice cream, oh, the flavors we choose!
With sprinkles and giggles, we run round the bend,
Making messes, not worries; it's fun with a friend.

We build silly castles from soft and warm sand,
With moats filled with jellybeans, all beautifully planned.

Yet when it all crumbles, we just choose to grin,
For laughter's the treasure we find deep within.

## The Bloom of Silent Assurances

In gardens of nonsense, we plant our wild dreams,
Pineapples on trees? Yes, or so it seems!
With baskets of giggles, we march through the scene,
As bubbles float higher, like floating cuisine.

We toss silly wishes on whims of the breeze,
And watch as they twist, like very odd keys.
In this wacky world where absurdity reigns,
We cling to the laughter that bursts through our veins.

## Whimsical Whispers

In the twilight's glow, our shadows engage,
Commencing a dance, pure absurdity's stage.
With socks on our hands, we wave to the moon,
In a spectacle crafted for just us, who knew?

With giggles as melodies, we sing off-key,
While balancing spoons on our noses with glee.
We sketch out a tale under stars oh-so-bright,
Finding joy in the odd, in our silly delight.

## **Echoes of the Unfurling**

A flower sneezed; oh, what a scene,
Balloons of color, pure and keen.
They tumbled down the garden path,
Chasing ants, inviting laughs.

Sunshine giggled, tickling grass,
While bees debated, 'Who's the sass?'
With every bloom, a secret flair,
Nature's jest, floating in the air.

## The Timeless Embrace

In springtime's arms, the bulbs all joke,
Hopping high like a playful folk.
Daffodils wearing hats so bright,
Say, 'We're the stars of the daylight!'

Tulips spin in a dance so grand,
While violets giggle, hand in hand.
They swear that days would never cease,
If laughter was the only lease.

## Secrets Within the Green

In a tangled mess of leafy curls,
The ants are plotting world of swirls.
Every twig a tale to tell,
Of garden gnomes who wish them well.

Whispers of daisies, oh so bright,
'Did you hear about that fly last night?'
A hiccup from the blooms nearby,
With every breeze, they laugh and sigh.

## Heartbeats Amongst the Leaves

Amidst the rustling, there's a cheer,
As ladybugs drink their evening beer.
While sparrows debate the best dessert,
With crumbs of laughter sure to flirt.

The wind plays harp through boughs so deep,
While creatures dance before they sleep.
Each heartbeat in this leafy maze,
Sings a tune of whimsical days.

## Between the Blooms and the Sky

In the garden, bees wear hats,
Dancing 'round like silly spats.
Flowers giggle, twist, and sway,
Chasing bugs who lost their way.

Sunlight plays a game of peek,
Winds are laughing — oh so cheek!
Dandelions blow wishes true,
While worms debate, 'What shall we do?'

## Eternal Yesterdays

Time is stuck in mud and clay,
Yesterday keeps wanting play!
Squirrels argue 'bout their stash,
While I just hope for a sweet snack.

Roses wink, with secret cheer,
While violets form a pious leer.
Every glance is pure delight,
As squirrels trip in playful flight.

## Garden of Quiet Resolutions

In the tangle, thoughts collide,
Bunnies hide to avoid the ride.
Violets vow to bloom with flair,
As hedgehogs plot a brave affair.

Whispers rustle through the leaves,
A wayward cat, a thief who weaves.
Each pledge is made with great delight,
Unless, of course, it rains tonight!

## The Charm of Unseen Alliances

A parade of ants in shoes,
Sneaking snacks and sharing news.
Each flower shares a hearty laugh,
While slimy slugs run out of path.

The ladybugs hide from the sun,
Plotting mischief just for fun.
In this charming wacky place,
Life's a game of silly grace.

## Glimmers of Light in the Shade

In the garden where daisies dance,
Lies a rabbit with a wayward stance.
He told a joke, oh what a grin,
But forgot the punchline, where to begin!

Sunflowers tower, bold and tall,
While listening mice are having a ball.
They giggle and squeak, sharing their snacks,
As butterflies plot little comical hacks.

A ladybug sports a hat quite grand,
Waving his wand, a wand so unplanned.
He tried to cast magic with a swoosh,
But instead tripped over a cheerful bush!

Beneath the blooms, frogs croak and tease,
Making the breeze giggle with ease.
They croon to the moon in a hearty song,
And promise the night won't be too long.

## Tender Roots of Connection

In a garden filled with quirky glee,
Two worms decided to sip on tea.
They wiggled and jiggled in cozy delight,
While sharing tales till the fall of night.

Under a toadstool, a snail moves slow,
He's writing a book, don't you know?
His plot's full of twists, and probably lies,
But everyone loves how the story flies!

A wise old owl with glasses perched,
Is coaching a squirrel who fumbles, then lurches.
"Just gather your nuts, don't go for a snack,
Or you'll end up rethinking your whole stack!"

When the sun dips low and shadows play,
The critters all gather for one last hooray.
With laughter that echoes, we share our treats,
In this quirky place, where silliness meets.

# Fragments of Floral Dreams

In the garden, ants parade,
Wearing hats that they have made.
Sunflowers bow with cheeky grace,
Daring bees to join the race.

Tulips gossip in the breeze,
Whispering about the tease.
Laughing leaves in shades of green,
Skate on dew like it's a scene.

Roses giggle, petals fluff,
Teasing stems, they're just so tough.
Daisies play a game of hide,
Creeping critters, tiny pride.

A dainty dance, the daisies sway,
Chasing shadows, come what may.
In this patch of funny lore,
Nature laughs forevermore.

## Secrets Beneath the Canopy

Under leaves of leafy jest,
Squirrels plot their little fest.
Bouncing on the boughs with flair,
Birds are judges at the fair.

Mushrooms mimicking a pie,
Wonder how the spiders fly?
Laughter rings from sun to shade,
Nature's joke, all nature made.

Fern fronds tease the morning light,
Rustling softly, oh what a sight!
Bumblebees in suits of gold,
Whisper secrets, brave and bold.

Grinning grasshoppers afar,
Joke about the fallen star.
In this realm of green delight,
Joyful whispers fill the night.

## **Threads of Nature's Pledge**

In the weave of floral schemes,
Worms conspire with wild dreams.
Butterflies don coats of bright,
Swirling in a dizzy flight.

Grass grows taller day by day,
Mischief blooms in every ray.
Thorns debate their point of view,
As petals giggle, bright and new.

A clumsy caterpillar slips,
Telling tales of flower trips.
Dandelions laugh out loud,
Wearing crowns that make them proud.

Nature's thread, such silly knots,
Plants and critters, funny thoughts.
In this garden, life's a stage,
Holding secrets age by age.

## **Echoes in the Bloom**

Nearby blooms yell "check it out!",
In a hushed, enthusiastic shout.
Vines entwine and giggle soft,
While petals float and drift aloft.

Crickets jump to rhythm's beat,
Making music, oh so sweet.
Sunset paints the sky in pranks,
While daisies dance in cheerful ranks.

Bewildered beetles roll on through,
Racing past the morning dew.
In the chaos, joy remains,
As laughter flows through leafy veins.

Breezes share their playful tales,
Rustling leaves like gentle gales.
In this bloom of life's own tune,
Echoes brighten afternoon.

## A Journey Through Petal Rain

In a world of flying bits,
Flowers dance and make a fit.
Breezes laugh and carry high,
Ticklish blooms that pass on by.

I slipped on one and did a swirl,
Thought I'd twirl, oh what a whirl!
Laughter echoed through the green,
As nature giggled, quite unseen.

Bouncing blooms in colors bright,
Throwing off their fragrance light.
A bee with flair dropped by to tease,
He buzzed the jokes with utmost ease.

Rain of petals, what a sight!
Who knew flowers could ignite?
With every step, I'm caught in glee,
This floral joke is just for me!

## Beacons of New Beginnings

A daisy dreams of shining bright,
Wishing on the stars tonight.
But then a squirrel, oh what a sight,
Dove into its leafy height!

"Hey there buddy, watch your fluff!"
The daisy sighed, "That's quite enough!"
The squirrel chuckled, filled with might,
"Let's share a laugh and ignite!"

New dawn breaks with silly schemes,
Sunshine leaks through all the seams.
The flowers plot a joyful prank,
A sneeze from me, and oh how they dank!

From tiny buds to vibrant show,
Each guarantees a funny flow.
When life gives you goofy nights,
Dance in petals, oh what delights!

## Blooming with Intention

Springtime turns the world to jest,
With flowers sprouting at their best.
A rose today wrote a note,
To say, "I'm the one with the coat!"

The lilies laughed, "Oh what a dream!
You think you're grand? You just gleam!"
They point and giggle, oh what fun,
In this garden where jokes run!

Intentions bloom in colors bold,
As each petal's story is told.
The tulips joke, "Guess we'll be late,
We can't stop blooming, just can't wait!"

From dirt to giggles, watch us grow,
Sprung from seeds with wit in tow.
Join the fun, no need for tension,
Life's a bloom, let's crack the mention!

## **Shades of Serendipity**

In a field of colors wild,
A sunflower winked, like a child.
"It's not just sun, it's also shade,
Where all the laughter's truly made!"

A butterfly flitted, tipsy and bright,
Like a comedian, taking flight.
"Do you think I'll land on that shoe?"
The daisies laughed, "Don't be a fool!"

When blooms collide, oh what a show,
They gather 'round with jokes that flow.
One dandelion, full of sass,
Declared, "Let's have a silly class!"

So bloom away in shades of cheer,
For nature's giggles wait right here.
With every rustle, a punchline's near,
In the garden, let's spread good cheer!

## The Softness of Sworn Hearts.

In gardens where whispers play,
Silly flowers have much to say.
With giggles that bloom all around,
They wear their bright colors, so proud!

Bees tease the daisies in a race,
Each petal grins in its own space.
A buttercup declares, "Behold!"
As ants march by, feeling quite bold!

Yet roses sigh with dear complaint,
Their thorns declare, "We're not a saint!"
Still, laughter snores beneath the sun,
Where seeds of whimsy come undone!

So dance within this fragrant spree,
Where hearts bloom wild, as wild can be.
And if you twirl, don't lose a shoe,
For nature's laughter waits for you!

## Whispers of Blossoms

In secret nooks where daisies joke,
Sunflowers giggle; oh, what a poke!
Carnations plan a prank on bees,
While lilacs whisper, "Oh, jeez!"

Tulips tease with colors so bright,
They bounce around, such a funny sight.
"Gotcha!" they shout as petals unfurl,
A pop of laughter in the swirl!

The violets huddle, sharing a laugh,
Plotting mischief for the nearby path.
Laughter erupts from every hue,
As nature's canvas comes alive, too!

So come along, embrace the cheer,
In this silly garden, have no fear!
With whispers of blooms and a dash of fun,
You'll find the joy where all began!

## The Garden of Unspoken Vows

In a garden where secrets hide,
Funny thoughts twist and collide.
Tulips wiggle with cheeky delight,
As petals quip, "What a sight!"

Dandelions puff with naughtiness,
Blowing wishes with such bliss.
"Let's promise to dance till the dawn!"
While crickets join, singing along!

A marigold grins, revealing a plan,
To turn garden gnomes into a band.
As bees form a chorus, low and sweet,
The flowers sway, tapping their feet!

So waltz with the wind, dance with a grin,
In the garden's embrace, let the laughter win!
For unspoken vows may flutter and sway,
But fun in this patch is here to stay!

### Dances in the Dew

Beneath the glow of the rising sun,
Silly droplets of dew have fun.
Each blades' dance is a splash of joy,
In this morning ballet, oh boy!

Grasshoppers leap, twirling in glee,
While whispers arise from the tall leafy tree.
Every flower spins, with laughter so bright,
Creating a scene of pure delight!

Butterflies flit, joining the spree,
With a hum that teases, "Follow me!"
A jolly waltz on the breeze so fine,
In this merry garden, everything shines!

So twirl 'neath the sun, where laughter is free,
And sip from the smiles of nature's decree.
For moments like this, always fresh and new,
Are dances we cherish, sprouted from dew!

## The Veil of Blossoms

In a garden, colors clash,
Butterflies plotting a daring flash.
Bees gossip in buzz and hum,
While silly ants think they're so glum.

A daisy bets it can outshine,
A rose with attitude so divine.
Tulips giggle at secrets shared,
Here's hoping no one is too scared!

## Unwritten Assurances

Promises written in the air,
Dandelions wish they could dare.
With every gust, a wish takes flight,
But they still can't find a pen that's right.

Fragrance dances, scents collide,
Jasmine's plans, oh how they slide!
Sunflowers plotting their next prank,
A garden party at the bank!

## Morning Glories and Silent Vows

Morning glories creep and climb,
Whisper jokes, oh so sublime.
With nodding heads, they plot mischief,
While bees, confused, just need a lift.

A daffodil grins, takes the lead,
To paint a scene with happy seed.
Yet vines twist jokes in every span,
A silly world made for a fan!

## The Heart's Garden

In the heart where laughter grows,
Silly secrets everyone knows.
A lily winks, a tulip pouts,
Caught in a dance of funny bouts.

Petunias play tag, round and round,
While sunbeams glow without a sound.
A thrumming tune, a joyous spree,
Who knew flowers could dance with glee?

## Whispers of Blooming Vows

In the garden of giggles, they sprout,
Wearing their colors, they jump about.
Under the sun, they twirl and tease,
Making bold claims that float with ease.

With a wink, they nod, a cheeky dance,
Each colorful hue takes a crazy chance.
Whispering secrets in the bright air,
It's hard to believe they don't have a care.

Like sneaky squirrels in a silly race,
Their laughter spreads, a charming embrace.
Bouncing in colors, they play and cheer,
Daring the winds to linger here.

As they spin tales of whimsical flair,
Petals prance lightly, hanging in air.
A promise made with a cheeky grin,
Who needs a vow when laughter's the win?

## Fragile Hues of Hope

Look at me, a yellow giggle, so bright,
Wrapped in green, what a funny sight!
I promise you laughter, I swear I bloom,
In this patch of dreams, there's always room.

A pink blush, oh so shy and pure,
With stammering hearts, we feel so sure.
Giggles and whispers, a riot of cheer,
Hope's fragile hues, that make it so clear.

In every breeze, there's a tickle and tease,
Colors collide, like a funny squeeze.
Swirling and dancing, under the sun,
Creating a ruckus, just for fun.

We don our colors, laughing with glee,
A cacophony of hues, wild and free.
In the garden of dreams, we joyfully cope,
Eagerly sharing our fragile hope.

## The Silent Oath of Blossoms

With a wink, the buds quietly bloom,
In the silence, there's mischief and room.
I solemnly swear, with petals in tow,
To spread joy around wherever I go.

Oh, look at that daisy, pitching a fit,
It sways side to side, what a little spit!
Proclaiming its vows with a giggling hush,
In the flower field, there's quite the rush.

Each bloom has a story, a quirky affair,
Whispered amongst leaves without a care.
Though rooted in soil, they wander and play,
Skipping around in a colorful fray.

So here's to the blossoms, with secrets to keep,
Beneath the bright sun, they dance and leap.
Locking their oaths in foolish delight,
With laughter as vows, they bloom day and night.

## **Tides of Spring's Commitment**

As springtime rolls in, a chuckle unfolds,
Colorful shenanigans, daring and bold.
With breezy whispers, they plot and scheme,
Creating a tide that dances with dreams.

Waves of giggles ripple in the air,
Every flower swaying without a care.
Giggling together, they form a crew,
Making promises that seem oh so true.

Each hue takes a plunge, splashing around,
In this sea of laughter, where joy is found.
With petals for floats, they bob and weave,
In a cycle of fun, what a gasp, what a cleave!

As the sun sets low, they share a wink,
Frolicking freely, they never rethink.
In the tides of jest, their vows take flight,
With laughter as unity, they dance into night.

## A Silent Accord

In the garden where secrets hide,
A gnome whispers, he's quite the guide.
With a wink, he stirs the herbs just right,
Claiming they spark dreams each night.

The carrots dance when no one's around,
They put on shoes and leap off the ground.
Tomatoes giggle, their laughter loud,
As bees throw parties, buzzing proud.

## The Garden of Hearts Unseen

Love blooms when the sun takes a break,
Roses wearing hats, for goodness' sake!
Tulips debate their colors with flair,
While daisies gossip without a care.

Bumblebees mix up their dance routine,
Trying to woo a shy tangerine.
With each flower, a story unfolds,
In this patch where imagination molds.

## Echoes of Tomorrow's Bloom

A sunflower winks, oh what a tease,
Swaying gently in the warm summer breeze.
Dandelions wish on old fluff balls,
Hoping someday to bounce off the walls.

Petunias plot a great escape,
On a quest to find a new landscape.
Chasing butterflies, they start to spin,
Laughs explosion underneath their skin.

## Bonds in Nature's Embrace

In the meadow, friendship takes root,
With daisies sharing their best fruit.
The violets giggle, tease the grass,
As ants march in, a tiny brass.

Squirrels hold a comedy night,
Telling tales of their wild flight.
With acorns as hats, they dance with glee,
In this quirky world, just wait and see.

## The Heart's Secret Blooms

In the garden, I found a sock,
It whispered secrets of a rock.
The daisies giggled, so did I,
As bees practiced their dance in the sky.

With each step, my shoes would squeak,
A silly tune that made me weak.
The daisies winked, the sun gave a cheer,
While butterflies laughed, 'What brings you here?'

Love's a tumble, a silly game,
Like trying to catch a wild flame.
With every giggle, the heart skips a beat,
As I trip over laughter, life's laughter is sweet.

So let love bloom in the oddest of places,
Like mismatched pairs or funny faces.
In the garden of jest, we'll play our part,
Where the truth of the heart is a joke with art.

## Silent Vows in the Breeze

Two squirrels chattered, plotting a plan,
While I daydreamed of making a man.
With acorns and leaves as our wedding cake,
Whispered secrets beneath the oak for fun's sake.

The wind teased whispers, a soft little dance,
As if tying my hopes with a whimsied chance.
Birds nodded along, with a cheerful good luck,
While I tripped over roots, oh what a cluck!

Promises fluttered in the air so light,
Like wishes cast on a starry night.
Yet here I am, flailing like a fish,
Lost in daydreams and an acorn dish.

In the hush of a breeze, my heart had its say,
Though squirrels are masters of love every day.
With laughter and mischief, we'll sway just right,
And cherish the humor in love's playful flight.

## Renewal in the Season's Embrace

Last winter's snow got lost in the sun,
A search party sent for the season's fun.
With tulips in shoes and daffodils in hats,
I danced through the garden, twirling with cats.

Springtime giggles rang through the air,
As I waved at the bunnies, unaware.
They frowned at my moves, a strange little sight,
While I tried to impress with a hop and a flight.

Gifts from the ground, oh how they bloom,
Yet I tripped on a weed, causing a boom.
With flowers in hand, all fragrant and bright,
Who knew love's fun can bring such a fright?

With each laugh I grow, so silly and true,
In the dance of the seasons, it's me and you.
Let's savor this mess, these quirks we embrace,
As love's true renewal is found in the chase.

## **Fleeting Glimmers of Affection**

A puddle reflected a silly face,
With wiggled eyebrows, I entered the race.
Bouncing like frogs, through rain and delight,
Each splash became laughter, oh what a sight!

Butterflies flitted, creating a scene,
As I chased after love like a goofball queen.
With dreams made of clouds and hopes made of cheer,
I giggled at every small slip of the year.

Arguments stirred like wild winds in May,
Yet hearts found a rhythm, a wobbly sway.
As leaves cascaded, we fell on the ground,
In a symphony of giggles—a love that astounds.

So here's to the moments that make us collide,
In this clumsy parade, our hearts open wide.
With each fleeting glimmer, let's dance in delight,
For laughter and love shine the brightest in flight.

## Glimpses of Tomorrow's Surrender

In the garden where squirrels play,
A gnome lost his hat on a sunny day.
Rabbits hop in a dance so sly,
As butterflies stare, they can't help but sigh.

The daisies gossip, oh what a scene,
While the tulips argue who's the queen.
A bumblebee stumbles, buzzes away,
Chasing dreams of nectar, come what may.

Lawn chairs wobble, just like our plans,
A shake of the head in the bushy fans.
Who knew tomorrow could be so bright,
With grass stains and laughter, and pure delight.

So what if we tumble, and trip on our toes?
Life's just a game, with its highs and lows.
Embrace the silly, let your heart race,
For the fun is in living, not just in the chase.

## The Resilient Garden of Belief

In a plot where veggies yell in delight,
Tomatoes wear caps, feeling quite right.
Carrots in shades, basking in light,
With radishes chuckling, oh what a sight!

The zucchini's a joker with jokes to spare,
While peppers are plotting, a dance in the air.
Each leaf contains laughter, a twist of good cheer,
As flowers all gossip about last year's flare.

With sprouts sporting helmets, so brave yet so green,
The onions are murmuring, discreet and unseen.
Fungi are giggling at all of it now,
As nature's own circus continues to wow.

So here's to the garden, its winks and its grins,
Where every small triumph is counted as wins.
Let's raise a wild cheer for this marvelous scene,
Where nature and laughter reign ever so keen.

## Blessings in the Breeze

The wind whispers secrets, so playful and light,
Tickling the leaves in a levity fight.
A kite sails by, nosedives so bold,
Telling a story that never gets old.

Pinecones are chuckling, right up in the trees,
As nutty acorns dance in the breeze.
Laughter of robins, a sweet serenade,
While breezes deliver the jokes they've made.

Clouds drift like pillows, lazy and free,
Painting pictures of whimsy for you and for me.
Each gust is a promise, a wink from above,
Wrapping the world in a hug full of love.

So let's spin like dandelions, wide-eyed and wild,
Chasing the laughter that nature has smiled.
Join in the frolic, let your spirit tease,
For joy is a treasure found in the breeze.

## Hearts in Bloom Amongst Shadows

In the twilight where shadows dance and sway,
Hearts pop like popcorn, come what may.
A lawn flamingo in a tutu spins,
While we lose our worries with innocent grins.

The breeze plays tag with the stars up so high,
Lighting up laughter, oh me, oh my!
Moonbeams are giggling, casting soft light,
While crickets serenade the Friday night.

Laughter erupts from the corner so neat,
Where shadows of lilies gather to meet.
With every quick quip, the world feels so bright,
Even the owls join in on the flight.

So gather your joy, in this whimsical land,
With hearts ever playful, hand in hand.
The night is our canvas, let laughter bloom,
In gardens of giggles, dispel every gloom.

## Threads of Eternal Spring

In gardens bright, a maze set wide,
Where daisies dance and giggles hide.
A sunflower winks, oh what a tease,
While bunnies hop and squirrels freeze.

The bees all hum a silly tune,
While daisies sway, they're in the moon.
A robin jokes, "I'm quite the catch!"
And blooms reply, "You're just a hatch!"

With every bloom, a laugh takes flight,
As petals chase the stars at night.
They joke about the winter's chill,
While prancing round, they dance at will.

Oh, nature's jest, so sweet and bright,
The blossoms play till dawn's first light.
In every wink, in every fling,
The joy of life is spring's grand king.

## The Silence Between the Flowers

Among the blooms, a secret grows,
A daisy turns and softly glows.
"Did you hear?" it whispers low,
"When tulips tango, oh they show!"

The roses giggle, their velvet red,
And chuckle soft of words unsaid.
While lilies sway in graceful dreams,
They laugh at all the silly schemes.

A buttercup bursts with laughter bright,
Saying, "Wait, am I yellow or white?"
And violets blush, they can't decide,
If they're shy, or just flower-pride.

In rustling leaves, the jokes unwind,
Each bloom a jester, well-defined.
Though soft and sweet, they're quite the crowd,
In the silence, their laughter's loud.

## A Dance of Love's Reflection

In a meadow where sunshine beams,
A couple of daisies share their dreams.
They twirl and laugh, they spin around,
In their own world, where joy is found.

"Oh darling bud," one said so grand,
"Together we'd make quite a flower band!"
With petals bright, they give a whirl,
While bees all swoon, "Now that's a twirl!"

A dandelion joins the fun,
"Look at me, I'm number one!"
They puff and cheer, a windy spree,
As pollen flies, "Come dance with me!"

With every leap and every spin,
The laughter bubbles from within.
A dance of love, both pure and true,
Among the blooms, there's always new.

## Traces of Yesterday's Sighs

In the garden where shadows fade,
A petal dropped, a memory made.
"Oh dear," sighed one, "that was my date!"
As blooms recount their whims and fate.

A tulip sighs, "Remember me?
With vibrant hues, so wild and free?"
The daisies laugh, "You were so bold!
With tales of love, or so we're told."

The sunflowers fade in the evening's glow,
Recalling moments from long ago.
"Did we really dance on the breeze?"
"Or was it just a game of tease?"

But laughter rings through tangled vines,
Where every sigh a joy defines.
So come, let's giggle at yesterday's trails,
In every whisper, the laughter prevails.

## The Spiral of Commitment

In circles we twirl, oh what a dance,
With funny mishaps, and a fleeting chance.
You trip on my shoelace, I spill my waste,
But here we are laughing, no time to waste.

We vow to be faithful, we promise to cheer,
Like socks on a summer day, we persevere.
The cake is a lie, but the fun's so real,
We toast to our fumbles, oh what a deal!

With every new twist, there's more to explore,
Like finding more fries hidden at the core.
Our rhythm's a waltz, both silly and grand,
We're bound by our stumbles, hand in hand.

So let's twirl again, in circles we'll roam,
Our love's a wild theme park, call it our home.
With clowns and balloons—a carnival sight,
In the spiral of commitment, everything's right.

## Blossom's Gentle Whisper

A flower once whispered, 'Hey, look at me!'
With petals of laughter, like odd comedy.
It danced in the breeze, a mischievous sight,
But ended up stuck, on a bird's wing, quite tight.

It promised to grow straight, oh what a fib!
Instead, it leaned crooked, who knew it could jib?
With roots in the wrong plot and sun in retreat,
Blossom just chuckled, 'This is my beat!'

The garden's a circus, a riot of cheer,
Where daisies tell jokes while the roses just sneer.
With bees as the audience, they buzz with delight,
As blossoms keep cracking their jokes day and night.

So let's paint our garden with laughter and cheer,
Where each bloom sings a tune for all to hear.
In every soft whisper and every twist here,
Let's gather our joy like a bouquet, my dear!

## Urban Gardens, Hidden Hopes

Amidst city chaos, there sprouts a dream,
With weeds on the block, and a squirrel named Cream.
We plant little seeds in a crack by the wall,
In hopes they'll bloom bright, though they might stall.

A sprout peeks tentatively, with giggles and glee,
Hiding from traffic, it longs to be free.
With pigeons throwing shade, and sunshine on lease,
Urban gardens hold stories, both silly and sweet.

The flowers are cheeky, they wave while we stroll,
And tickle our fancies, playfully whole.
Hidden hopes flourish in concrete's embrace,
As we dance with our dreams, in this busy place.

Let's laugh at the sidewalks, let's cheer at the grime,
For in every small bud, there's a rhythm, a rhyme.
In the heart of the city, where chaos won't stop,
We'll grow roots of joy, till the last bubble pops.

## **A Harmony of Soft Colors**

In the shades of the garden, a color parade,
With mauve and with mint, and lemonade played.
They giggle and sing, as they sway in the breeze,
Chasing each other, oh, won't you join, please?

The yellow blooms whistle, while blue ones just smirk,
In a melody spinning, with each bold little quirk.
They chat about sunshine, about winner's delight,
While lying together, in soft, warm moonlight.

Small butterflies chuckle, as they flit about,
Tracing dainty paths, with a giggly shout.
Each hue has a secret it whispers at night,
In this harmony sweet, there's a splash of pure light.

So here's to the laughter, to colors that play,
In gardens of whimsy, let's dance through the day.
For life's just a canvas, a palette to share,
In a world full of joy, let's color everywhere!

## **Roots of Promised Connection**

In a garden of quirks, we both did bloom,
Ropes of laughter wrapped, chasing gloom.
With silly secrets woven tight,
We sprout and twist, a curious sight.

When weeds of doubt attempt to grow,
We laugh and pull out each little toe.
Roots tickle the ground, they wiggle and sway,
Our playful bond brightens each day.

Sunshine whispers, 'Let's make a joke,'
While dance moves arise—oh, what a bloke!
In mud-stained shoes, we leap and bound,
With goofy smiles, joy can be found.

So here's to our sprouts, both silly and spry,
Winking at clouds wandering dry.
In this garden of life, let's forever stay,
As dance partners on this fun-filled way.

## Dance of the Blossoming Hearts

In a field of chuckles, our antics fly,
With wiggly moves that defy the shy.
We twirl in circles, our giggles align,
Oh, what a scene, it's utterly fine!

A snort here, a hop there, we rumble and roll,
In the blushing sunlight, we soak up the whole.
Our hearts do a jig as the breeze joins our fun,
Like flowers in bloom, racing towards the sun.

Step on my toes, I'll dance on your feet,
With melodies weird, our rhythms repeat.
Forget fancy moves, just follow your thrill,
In this frolicsome show, let's share a huge hill!

With shadows entwined, we laugh till we ache,
In this bright ballet, there's nothing to fake.
So grab me and laugh as we pirouette here,
Forever entwined, let's spread endless cheer!

## **Wings of a Fresh Start**

With wings of humor, we soar and glide,
In the sky of laughter, let's take a ride.
Flip and flap, as we start anew,
With ticklish breezes that dance right through.

Each feather a joke, each breeze a cheer,
With comical skies, there's nothing to fear.
We flap through the clouds, tickling the sun,
As our silly hearts flutter, oh what fun!

With a wink and a jig, let's spread our delight,
In this zany adventure, we bask in the light.
We soar over fields of laughter and jests,
On wings made for giggles, we build our nests.

So come take a leap, let's spread our bright glee,
In this whimsical flight, we're wild and free.
A fresh start awaits as we rise with a cheer,
Embracing the joy of this joyful frontier!

## **Petal Soft Affections**

In a cuddly corner, we cozy and tease,
With whispers so sweet, they float on the breeze.
A poke and a hug, we jostle with joy,
As mishaps abound, like a clumsy boy.

With fluffy-eyed giggles, we snicker and play,
Our humor unwinds in a funny buffet.
Soft touches of laughter, like tickling rain,
In our playful embrace, we lose track of pain.

Serenades sung with a twist and a turn,
In this funny dance, we happily learn.
With a wink and a grin, it's a soft delight,
Affections abound in the heart of the night.

So let's flutter close, in this sweet design,
With ticklish affections that charmingly shine.
Through whims and fancies, let's giggle and sway,
In the warm light of humor, forever we'll play.

## **Flickers of Hope within Leaves**

Among the trees a squirrel danced,
Chasing shadows, in a trance.
Leaves above began to sway,
Wondering if it's time to play.

A butterfly with flair absurd,
Flashed by like a silly bird.
It winked and spun, a show-off bright,
Confusing bumblebees in flight.

Dandelions in a puff,
Spread their seeds; they just can't get enough.
With each gust, a giggling spree,
Floating dreams of what could be.

Underneath this leafy wave,
Laughter hides, oh what a rave!
Nature's jesters, wild and bold,
Weave a story yet untold.

## The Promise of Blossoming

In the garden, a snail moves slow,
Claiming territory, taking a bow.
A tulip giggles, its bud so tight,
Says, "I'll bloom, just wait for night!"

Ants march like tiny soldiers proud,
Making vows, quite unbowed.
They gather crumbs with zeal and cheer,
Promising feasts without a fear.

Roses whisper, "We'll soon compete!
Who can smell the best and sweet?"
In a twist, the daisies chime,
"Let's wear crowns, it's blooming time!"

With laughter and petals as confetti,
Sunny days, oh so very petty.
Each bloom a promise, oh what fun,
Let's dance in circles, one by one.

## A Chorus of Colorful Commitments

In the meadow where colors clash,
Fluffy clouds begin to splash.
Carnival blooms with laughter loud,
Enticing every passing crowd.

The lilacs vow to steal the show,
While daisies giggle, "We are in the flow!"
Zinnias join, all decked in flair,
Swirling blooms fill the air.

The sun peeks in, a playful tease,
Tickling buds with a gentle breeze.
Promises echo, bouncing high,
Worries scatter like a pinwheel's sigh.

Each color shines, a cheeky wink,
Nature's joke, don't you think?
A chorus of hues sings out loud,
Together we flourish, proud and unbowed.

## In the Shade of Floral Whispers

Beneath the blooms, a secret lies,
With giggling vines and watchful eyes.
Petunias gossip, sharing tales,
Of butterflies with silly gales.

A bumblebee, in a tux, so chic,
Dances clumsily, his moves unique.
"I promise to find the best bouquet,
If I can just make it through the day!"

Morning glories stretch and yawn,
Planning trickery at the dawn.
"Let's confuse the daffodils," they jest,
"Who can hide the best? A funny quest!"

In the shade of whispers, all agree,
Life is better with jests and glee.
A floral world, both bright and bold,
Tales of laughter too sweet to hold.

## The Unfurled Heart

In the garden of laughter, we twirl,
With puns and chuckles, our jokes unfurl.
Beneath the sun, we dance so bright,
Two silly souls, in pure delight.

You said you'd bring me ice cream cones,
But all I got were random bones!
Your promises sweetened, like a candy line,
Yet here I stand, with a pet dog whine.

We chase our shadows, silly and spry,
Trading whispers that never lie.
With giggles galore, we roll on the grass,
And laugh so hard, we scare the passers.

In this bright world of fun and cheer,
Our quirks unite, we shift and steer.
So here's to us, with joy, we blend,
Two jokesters' hearts, a perfect end.

## Radiance of Untold Oaths

In a field of giggles, we vowed to play,
To stick together, come what may.
You promised me sweets, a marshmallow hue,
But only got crumbs, oh what a view!

Those whispered secrets in the bright sun,
Not quite what I meant, but still quite fun.
With wildflowers in our hair and hearts so light,
We reenact tales, oh such a sight!

Our vows were like lemonade, sweet and tart,
Bubbling laughter, straight from the heart.
But who's gonna fix the blender, I plead?
You said you would, oh where's that speed?

Yet here we stand, like clowns in flight,
With silly grins and hearts so bright.
Who needs oaths in the air so free?
With you beside, it's pure jubilee!

## **Petal Soft Secrets**

In the twilight's giggle, we chat and scheme,
Sharing soft secrets, oh what a dream!
You say I'm a gem, but should I be gold?
With every promise, my smile unfolds.

You added some spice, but I want the sweet,
When it comes to desserts, can't be beat.
"Just one more slice!" I gleefully cry,
But your diet jokes make me sigh.

With a wink, we frolic, in shadows we hide,
Playing hopscotch while holding pride.
"Your shoes are too big!" you tease and then trip,
As our laughter erupts, on this joyous trip.

From whispered giggles to bubbly cheer,
In this funny bond, it's perfectly clear.
No secrets untold, just fun all around,
With every chuckle, pure joy is found.

## Echoes of a Gentle Promise

Whispers linger, as the sun dips low,
We share our dreams in a funny flow.
You pledged to tickle the clouds so high,
But here on Earth, you just made me cry!

"Let's cook dinner!" you shouted with glee,
But ended up frying my poor zucchini.
The smoke alerts, the fire alarm sings,
In our kitchen chaos, the laughter springs.

Chasing echoes of what could be ours,
In this dance of love, we twirl like stars.
Your whispered wants give way to delight,
All these mishaps make everything bright.

With goofy charms, we wander aimless,
In this world of mishaps, we're the famous.
So here's to our antics, forever and free,
Two hearts in sync, just you and me!

## Secrets Beneath Soft Shelters

In the garden, whispers bloom,
Worms gossip with gusto, filling the room.
A squirrel steals my sandwich near,
While daisies laugh, they're in on the cheer.

Bees wear tuxedos, buzzing so proud,
They dance on the flowers, entertaining the crowd.
Meadows are hiding that secret stash,
Of garden gnomes plotting their next great bash.

Frogs croak out tunes, conducting a symphony,
While grasshoppers strut like it's their epiphany.
I trip on a root, and the sun gives a wink,
Nature's a comedian, don't you dare blink!

Under leafy blankets, the secrets we share,
Chasing the critters, without a care.
And as the moon giggles overhead,
I'll never tell a soul what we've said!

## **Blooming Under Starlit Skies**

Stars above wink like mischief in flight,
While night blooms whisper, 'Is this wrong or right?'
Crickets play chess on the old wooden bench,
A hedgehog rolls past, avoiding the wrench.

The moon smiles wide, a silent cheerleader,
While fireflies twinkle, remind me to be sweeter.
They're dodging my dance, like they're in a race,
As I step on a worm, it's quite the disgrace!

Owls gossip loudly, like they own the night,
While I try to hush them, to keep it polite.
A raccoon joins in, wearing a mask of flair,
Stealing my snacks, as if I'm not there!

Under soft shadows, we laugh 'til we ache,
With nature's oddities, the fun we can make.
The dawn creeps in, it's time to retreat,
But tonight was amazing, no trip was too fleet!

## Threads of Love in Garden Paths

Tangled in ivy, two bunnies collide,
They hop around wildly, can't pick a side.
Ladybugs giggle, painted so bright,
As they tease the ants with a delightful fright.

Underfoot daisies play peek-a-boo fun,
With worms underground, plotting a run.
A dandelion whispers, 'Life is a joke,'
While I try to impress with my soft-spoken smoke.

A puppy runs through, causing a stir,
Chasing his tail, full of happy blur.
Overgrown weeds roll their eyes in disbelief,
While butterflies swoop for a chance at relief.

Crooked paths lead us to laughter and glee,
In this quirky garden, come, join me.
For love is a garden, tangled and free,
And every odd moment is just meant to be!

## **Echoes of Floral Reverie**

Upon a hill, blossoms bust out in song,
While bees keep the beat, they can do no wrong.
A wind chime giggles, swaying so light,
As daisies roll over, ready for night.

Tulips trade secrets, oh what a delight,
Whispering tales of the quirky moonlight.
The roses complain of their pricking, oh boy!
While sunflowers laugh, much too proud to be coy.

A frog on a lily, croaks a rude joke,
While skunks pass by, not caring who's woke.
Each petal a story, a monumental cheer,
In this floral rave, everyone's welcome here!

So let's dance in the garden, mischief alight,
Join the marigolds kicking with all of their might.
For in these echoes, our joy shall arise,
With laughter as fragrant as starlit skies!

## Shades of Trust in Nature's Embrace

In a garden where daisies play,
A squirrel thinks he's found his buffet.
He munches leaves with cheeky delight,
While ants march on, steadfast at night.

The trees gossip with the wind's soft sighs,
Laughing at clouds as they roll by.
Rabbits hop, nibbling at dreams,
As bees buzz out sweet, sticky schemes.

Sunflowers dance in a sunlit waltz,
While weeds poke fun at the garden's faults.
The earth chuckles at the rush of roots,
And flowers bicker over their cute suits.

So trust the whims of this lively show,
Watch nature's antics, and let joy grow!
In laughter's embrace, let hearts invade,
As every leaf spills secrets not made.

## Harmonies of the Cultivated Soul

In rows of veggies, a symphony starts,
Where radishes strum with joyful hearts.
The carrots hum a low, earthy tune,
While lettuce giggles under the moon.

A pumpkin pretends he's a royal king,
Wearing a crown made of celebration's ring.
He boasts of his seeds, all hearty and grand,
While marigolds play, lending a hand.

Herbs whisper sweet nothings in the breeze,
Enticing the chef with such tantalizing ease.
Oregano sways as thyme gives a wink,
In the kitchen's harmony, they steal the drink.

The garden's chorus of chuckles unfold,
With rhythms of pest control bravely bold.
Through laughter and flavors, hearts become whole,
In this quirky dance of the cultivated soul.

## The Canvas of Unspoken Devotion

In corners where shadows dare play hide and seek,
Lurks a painter with brushes, all vibrant and unique.
He daubs the air with splashes of cheer,
As flowers bloom just to stand and sneer.

A sunflower lifts with a twinkling grin,
While violets whisper secrets of where they've been.
The artist spills laughter on the canvas wide,
In colors of joy where silliness hides.

Each brushstroke jests, creating a scene,
Of blossoms that giggle, oh, what could it mean?
Bees buzz in sync, the music they know,
As daisies strike poses in sunshine's soft glow.

With sneaky strokes of a delightful plan,
The night sky listens to this floral band.
Devotion in colors both strange and divine,
In this playful art, hearts intertwine.

## Swirling Blooms of Aspiration

The daisies dream of dancing high,
While lilacs scheme to touch the sky.
A windy twist sends them spinning around,
As laughter erupts from the fertile ground.

Butterflies flutter, tiptoeing through air,
Stopping to gossip, they flair without care.
Each bloom, a tale of sweet silliness shared,
With petals all dressed, each one fairly geared.

Dandelions launch their fluffy white seeds,
With hopes they'll sprout in strange, silly breeds.
They giggle as gusts take them far and wide,
In swirling adventures of whimsy and pride.

So join in the frolic where dreams come alive,
In blossoms that giggle, so happy to thrive.
With aspirations flaring through nature's grand scheme,
The garden invites you to dance in the dream.

## Embracing the Fragile Moments

I once saw a flower, doing a jig,
It swayed to the breeze, oh so big!
"Don't crush me too hard," it said with a grin,
"I've got a dance-off with the wind to win!"

My vase is a stage, each bloom takes a turn,
In the spotlight they twist, oh how they yearn!
Every wilted petal, a tale of its own,
With rumors of bees trying to clone!

When tea comes to visit, the daisies get bold,
They gossip of sunshine, stories retold.
"Last week, did you see how the lilac got snagged?"
"Her dress was too bright, it left us all bragged!"

So here's to the moments, both fragile and bright,
A laugh with a daisy, what a glorious sight!
In the garden we giggle, life's truly a jest,
Embrace all the quirks; they're simply the best!

## Beneath the Canopy of Hope

Under the leaves where the squirrels conspire,
The daisies declare, "We'll never retire!"
They wiggle and giggle, in jubilant cheer,
Claiming each raindrop is just a cold beer!

A dandelion whispers, "I want to be bold,
To float through the clouds, or so I am told."
He dreams of adventures, with dreams full of flair,
Yet, missed the great flight, with a tumble and stare.

Sunflowers dance while they plan the next stunt,
"I'll spin 'round the corner, when called for a front!"
And all of the roses, just chuckle and sigh,
"Watch out for that breeze, or you'll kiss the sky!"

So gather your curls, and twirl with delight,
There's magic in laughter, in the morning light.
Under the foliage, where fun blooms and grows,
Life's silliness sparkles, in petals and prose!

## Sweet Conspiracies of the Heart

In the garden of whispers, where secrets convene,
The violets huddle, they're quite the keen scene.
"Did you hear about Betty?" they chuckle and snicker,
"Her fragrance was bold, and oh, what a flicker!"

Carnations are plotting their painting parade,
While lupines discuss the performances made.
"Let's bluff all the bugs, make them dance in a row,
While we sip on the dew, and put on a show!"

A lilac just giggles, "Let's hide all the bells!
They'll think it's a party, oh how they'll yell!"
With mischief afoot, and petals aglow,
The romance of friendship continues to flow.

In this charming retreat, love twirls on its toes,
Laughing through silence, where the heart truly knows.
So here's to the blooms, with secrets to chart,
A shenanigan fest, full of love from the heart!

## In the Midst of Unfurling

A bud took a chance, stretched wide in the sun,
"I'm ready to thrive, let the unrolling fun!"
But as it revealed, out popped a snail,
"Excuse me, dear flower, you're blocking my trail!"

The blossoms all chuckled, this was quite the show,
"Hey, don't take it hard; there's room here to grow!"
But that wily old snail, with a wink and a grin,
Replied, "I've got plans; let the race begin!"

With petals in laughter, they gathered their friends,
Figuring out how this rivalry ends.
"Let's roll down the hill! Sort out all the fuss!"
While dandelions murmured beneath all the dust.

When flowers unite, with the humor of spring,
Life's really a party, come join in and sing!
In the frost of the night, with the sun soon to call,
It's the antics of blooms that conquers us all!

## Seeds of Affection in Gentle Soil

In a garden of giggles, we plant our dreams,
With watering cans full of laughter beams.
We sprinkle our wishes, see them take flight,
As weeds in the corner plot dance in delight.

A sunflower whispers, 'You look like a snack!'
While daisies debate the best color of slacks.
We clash with the critters who steal our snacks,
Yet tend to our quirks with friendly, warm quacks.

We dig little trenches and pull up the roots,
Share stories with worms in our goofy old boots.
Under moonlit skies, we chat with the bugs,
Laughing at all of our awkward old hugs.

So here's to the soil where our goofy love grows,
With seeds of affection, and everyone knows.
In this funny little patch, we bloom and we play,
Building sweet memories, day after day.

## Rich Tones of Unfaltering Bonds

Two friends on a swing, both with ice cream cones,
Laughing at all of the silly old tones.
With laughter as currency, we're rich as can be,
Sharing secrets that make us both giggle with glee.

We jam to the rhythm of clumsy old tunes,
As frogs join the chorus beneath crescent moons.
In our world of bananas and jelly-filled pies,
Every tiny mishap draws curious sighs.

A dance on the lawn brings the neighbors to stare,
With gardening gloves, we declare, 'We don't care!'
Riding on tricycles, we paint the town red,
With bold strokes of chaos, our worries will shed.

No matter how tangled our pathways may get,
We hold onto friendship without any fret.
Wrapped in our laughter, the canvas is bright,
Painting rich bonds in the soft morning light.

## The Elegance of Shared Secrets

Underneath the grand oak, conspirators meet,
Sharing wild dreams over strawberries sweet.
We giggle in whispers, our heads all in gear,
Crafting strange legends that only we hear.

With crackers and cheese, and a hint of a dare,
We scheme for the cookies that sit in the air.
The squirrels listen closely, a twitch in their tails,
As we spin tall tales about dragon-flavored gales.

A handshake of jelly, a pact made with cheer,
As we promise to laugh through each tiny fear.
With sunshine as witness, we dash off the plot,
Beneath oversharing, we give it a shot.

So here's to our secrets, all silly and bright,
In the heart of the woods, all the wrongs turn to right.
We'll dance with our quirks, be as goofy as can be,
Sharing elegance found in our beautiful spree.

## **Illuminated by Nature's Touch**

In the glow of the fireflies, we swing in delight,
Plotting to prank all the bugs with our fright.
With cookie-bribed crickets; 'Don't play it too loud,'
We whirl through the meadows, our laughter, a crowd.

The frogs croak their tunes, like a band out of time,
Each ribbit a note in our silly rhyme.
Budding our friendships under wild, starry skies,
While counting the hiccups and giggles, we rise.

With petals of laughter, we flutter about,
Creating a story that's funny, no doubt.
We gather sweet moments, let giggles be bold,
And treasure the wonders, like treasure of gold.

So let's chase the dusk with our hearts open wide,
For nature will cheer on this joyous wild ride.
With each twinkling spark, our friendship ignites,
In this dance of connections, we shine through the nights.

## The Dance of Colorful Agreements

In a garden full of quirk,
Where daisies wear their smirk,
Yellow yells, 'I'm the best!'
While reds compete like a jest.

Some argue with a wag of leaf,
Fighting for the silliest beef,
'I'm sprightly, bright, and quite a catch!'
Said the poppy with a scratch.

Then a dandelion piped in clear,
'This is my year, give me a cheer!'
Laughter swirls in floral delight,
As petals giggle through the night.

So they twirl, spin, and parade,
In a comical charade,
Their colorful jests, a vibrant show,
In the garden where laughter grows.

## **Beneath the Canopy of Wishes**

Underneath a leafy dome,
Wishes whisper, call it home,
Dreams hang like fruit so sweet,
Each hope a chuckle, a little treat.

A breeze tickles all that's there,
Tickling leaves, making them flare,
'You'll never grow too tall,' it claims,
As branches laugh and play their games.

Twinkling stars poke fun at fate,
'Hey, look at that funny date!'
Each wish takes flight with joyous glee,
Wobbling, wobbling, like a bee.

So here's to giggles in the night,
Where laughter dances, hearts take flight,
Underneath this leafy shade,
Wishes make a delightful trade.

## Vows Carried on the Breeze

A breeze flew by with vows so grand,
Tickling petals across the land,
'I swear I won't wilt before noon,'
Said the sunflower, laughing at the moon.

'I'll always lean this way for you!'
Chortled the daffodil, bright and true,
While violets shook their heads in glee,
'Oh please, we all know it's just for tea!'

Promises floated in the air,
With an aroma both rich and rare,
'We'll bloom together, that's the deal,'
Said the rose, striking a funny wheel.

So they wink and sway with grace,
In their humorous, flowery race,
Vows twirl in laughter, never a bore,
As breezes carry their silly lore.

## The Language of Flourishing Hearts

In a meadow where laughter grows,
A language blooms that no one knows,
With giggles pinned on every leaf,
And petals blushing in disbelief.

Yellow speaks in chirpy tones,
While lilacs chuckle, shaking bones,
'Why does blue think it's so cool?'
The daisies tease, 'You're such a fool!'

They trade sweet nods and twinkly winks,
In a language made of giggles and kinks,
Each bloom knows just when to jest,
As if the garden is one big fest.

So let the world in colors bright,
Join this laughter, pure delight,
For in this flowery, funny game,
Every heart shares a humorous name.

www.ingramcontent.com/pod-product-compliance
Lightning Source LLC
Chambersburg PA
CBHW072223070526
44585CB00015B/1460